AF605018

To mum, master of the power drill and fairy tale reads, stir fry sauces and triathlons. Thank you for always doing your best for us – and your grandkids – and doing it your way. – JR

First published in Australia in 2020 by Affirm Press, a Simon & Schuster (Australia) Pty Limited company

Bunurong/Boon Wurrung Country

28 Thistlethwaite Street, South Melbourne VIC 3205

Affirm Press is located on the unceded land of the Bunurong/Boon Wurrung peoples of the Kulin Nation.
Affirm Press pays respect to their Elders past and present.

New York Amsterdam/Antwerp London Toronto Sydney/Melbourne New Delhi

Visit our website at www.simonandschuster.com.au

20 19 18 17 16

A Cataloguing-in-Publication entry for this book is available
from the National Library of Australia

9781925972917 (hardback)

Cover design by Hannah Janzen
Printed and bound in China by C&C Offset Printing Co. Ltd.

Welcome Baby

to this world

Jess Racklyeft

Welcome, baby, to this world
Lashes long and fingers curled.
Dreaming stories for our years
Whispered words to tiny ears.

We'll build boats from
twigs and twine

Craft a castle we can climb

Treasure-hunt in golden grass
With clouds of secrets blowing past.

Every day I'll love you more
We'll skip round pebbles from the shore

Wrap warm in hugs when
winds blow cold

Go looking for the rainbow gold.

I'll lift you to those bendy trees
Sing songs to calm the wild bees.

Kiss better a bruised heart or knee

Brew lemon, mint and honey tea.

We'll plant a patch of rambling flowers
Rescue Dragon from King's tower.

Sail through worlds picked from a shelf

I’ll watch you, one day, read yourself.

Find my heart, it's stitched to yours

It’s waiting by your treehouse door

It's in the cupcakes that we'll bake

Slow gumboot walks that we will take.

Tides will rise and moons will fall
I'll be beside you, through it all.

I’ll make mistakes – you will too . . .

I’ll do my very best for you.

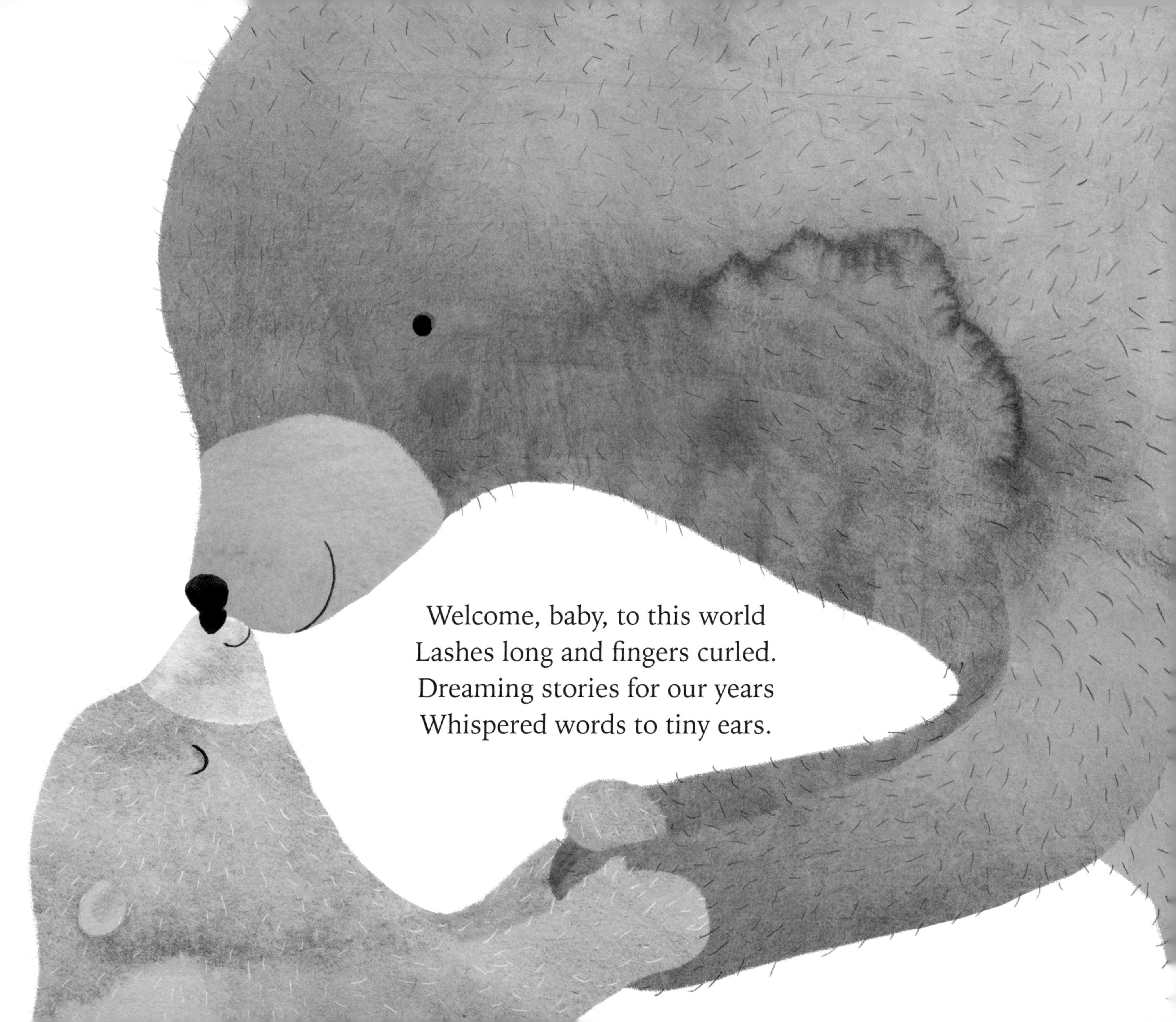

Welcome, baby, to this world
Lashes long and fingers curled.
Dreaming stories for our years
Whispered words to tiny ears.